weeds and W

D1180308

for: Dave and Jean

May God bless you richly and fill your garden with
love, joy and peace in every season...

from: Margaret.

Photo: Tim Sandall

Attention, all!
See the marvels of God!
He plants flowers and trees all over the earth...

Psalm 46:8 (The Message)

Weeds and wonders

The LORD himself goes before you and will be with you; he will never leave you nor forsake you. Do not be afraid; do not be discouraged.

Deuteronomy 31:8 (NIV)

●

Our new house came with a brand-new garden, a square of lawn surrounded on three sides by fencing with the house on the fourth side. The builders had laid the turf and then downed tools. In the early days, it was a very low-maintenance garden, since once the lawn had been given its weekly haircut, there was nothing left to do!

Over the years we carved out flower beds, planted trees, added a shed and a shrubbery, a patio and a Wendy House, and slowly the square of grass became *our* garden. Creating a garden from scratch was fascinating and it gave us a tiny taste of how God must have felt at the dawn of creation. *"God saw all that he had made, and it was very good."* Genesis 1:31 (NIV)

The plants made themselves at home, put down roots and sent up shoots. The clematis climbed, the petunias trailed and there was always something to wonder at or admire. Everything in the garden was rosy. And then… the weeds moved in and invited their friends! Those weeds blossomed and flourished, you couldn't fault their enthusiasm, but they were definitely gate-crashing the party.

We continue to fight a discouraging battle against ground-elder in the shrubbery, and dandelions and creeping thistles in the lawn. Where did they come from? Sometimes we're on top of the situation and sometimes the weeds have the upper hand. Life's a bit like that too, sometimes it's weedy and sometimes it's wonderful, but frequently a combination of both, rather like in the garden, where weeds and wonders grow side by side.

Trouble and stress comes into our lives uninvited, just like weeds. No matter how much you prepare and plan, life is sometimes less than perfect, but God knows and cares and he is with us in every circumstance, good and bad.

So talk to God about the tough times and thank him for the good times – and remember the old gardener's advice: *When the going gets tough, the tough get growin'*. Gardening is splendid, stress-busting therapy.

Lord, it's good to know that you're close by in the good times and bad. Remind us to reach out for your hand when the going gets tough, and to stay in touch when all's going well.

Photo: Ian Strachan

'Weeds are flowers too, once you get to know them,' said Eeyore.
A.A.Milne *1882–1956, creator of Winnie the Pooh*

Tight support

When I said, "My foot is slipping," your love, O LORD, supported me.
Psalm 94:18 (NIV)

●

Some years ago, a loud rustle followed by a dull thump made me run to the window and gaze down on our dark garden below. In the dawn light, I could just make out our eucalyptus tree, leaves down, roots up, in the wet grass. The stormy winds had brought down one of my favourite trees. Evergreen, fragrant and great for flower arrangements – you couldn't ask for much more from a tree. Tucking pyjamas into wellingtons, I rushed into the garden. The strap that bound the young tree to the support stake had broken and so the tree had been brutally swayed by the storm until it had finally fallen.

I had been given this eucalyptus as a sapling, fresh out of the nursery, and I wasn't about to lose it. Inside, I searched for something to tie the tree back to its stake. Then I had an idea... a pair of tights. I found an old, green pair of tights that had once given me the air of Kermit the Frog – they were just the thing, leaf-green and stretchy. I raised the eucalyptus to its normal position and tied the tights twice round the tree and the stake, *tightly* of course. These were now real support tights.

There are times when we all feel buffeted by a storm: redundancy, bereavement, ill health, divorce... the list is endless. And then we all need someone to wrap their arms around us and help us to remain standing. Many Christians have a real gift for supporting and listening to others. May God bless them richly. Is there someone you could reach out to today?

To cultivate a garden is to walk with God.
***Christian Nevell Bovee** 1820–1904, American Author and Lawyer*

Photo: Tim Sandall

Perhaps make a phone call, send an email, post a card or arrange some flowers for them, or maybe they just need a hug, a really *tight* hug.

And remember, if it's you that's being swayed by the storm, Jesus stretched out his arms and said 'I love you this much'.

Photo: Judith Merrell

Lord, thanks for the friends and family who support me when life is difficult, and thank you that you are ready to hold me tight as I ride out life's storms. When it's my friends that are in trouble, help me to show your love and support to them.

This is your garden, Creator God,
A thing of beauty
Beyond understanding.
A poem that is being written,
Not in words
But in colours,
Wind's whisper,
Soaring bird,
Snowdrop's petal,
Gentle rain,
Sunlight's warmth.
This is your garden, Creator God,
A thing of beauty
Beyond understanding.

John Birch

Snails don't have a reverse gear

Joyful is the person who finds wisdom, the one who gains understanding.
For wisdom is more profitable than silver, and her wages are better than gold.

Proverbs 3:13-14 (NLT)

I made a startling discovery the other day. It may not change the world but it's this: snails don't have a reverse gear. I went to the greenhouse to water my plants. The watering can was heavy, full of water, but when I picked it up and tilted it, only a trickle of water came through. I put the can down, unscrewed the spout and held it up to the light. It was almost totally blocked by something dark. I poked a cane through the narrow end and out dropped a snail. A dead snail.

Attracted by the damp, it must have crawled in and up the spout. Unfortunately, watering can spouts taper and get smaller nearer the outlet. The snail went in as far as it could go, then got jammed. And that was that. There was no room to turn and the snail had no reverse gear.

It made me think. Never put yourself in a situation you can't back out of. Bad grammar, but you see what I mean. People argue and, in the heat of the moment, make statements they can't justify, and then find they can't back away. Too embarrassing. They get aggressive, which makes things worse, and before you know it World War Three's broken out. Or nearly so.

Take time to listen to what the other person's saying. Put yourself in their place and don't push too hard or you may get stuck without any chance of backing away. Leave room for understanding and keep the channels of communication unblocked. Remember the snail.

By Eddie Askew, taken from *Love is a Wild Bird,*
published by The Leprosy Mission

Photo: Ian Strachan

Lord, it may be asking a lot of you, but help me to think before I speak, and then not to say too much.

Photo: Jonathan Merrell

No two gardens are the same. No two days are the same in one garden.

Hugh Johnson

Re-potting – a serious business

The Lord had said to Abram, "Leave your country, your people and your father's household and go to the land I will show you."

Genesis 12:1 (NIV)

●

Re-potting is one of my favourite gardening jobs. I enjoy the whole process, from preparing a fresh pot for a root-bound specimen, to watching it fill the space around it over the following weeks. I can almost picture the re-housed plant giving a sigh of contentment as it flexes its toes in fresh soil, luxuriating in the extra space.

God is also in the business of re-potting, though we Christians may find it an uncomfortable experience. God knows when we've outgrown our place or situation, so he moves us out of our comfort zone.

We don't often welcome the idea of being uprooted by God. We are creatures of habit. We grow accustomed to our pot, our role within our workplace, our church and our community. Even if we feel cramped and claustrophobic, we take heart from knowing who we are and what's expected of us in our current situation. But we stop growing in a pot that no longer fits, and a soil which has lost its nutrients. Bonsai Christians aren't what God wants.

When God does re-pot us, we can feel way out of our depth. Suddenly, we're in unfamiliar soil, perhaps feeling lost, small and insignificant. It takes a while for us to stretch out and appreciate the new experience. But once we recognise that God has planted us where we are for a reason, we can face new challenges with confidence, secure in the knowledge that God will tend us and that we will grow in his love to fill the new role he has given us.

PS: Don't expect a bonsai tree to grow the miniature planting it.

Lord, help us to face up to the new situations and challenges with which you present us. You know best where to plant us for strong, healthy growth. Thank you, Father.

GARDEN sayings

The Earth laughs in flowers.

Ralph Waldo Emerson *1803–1882, American writer and lecturer*

•

You're only here for a short visit. Don't hurry, don't worry, and stop to smell the flowers along the way.

Walter Hagen *1892–1969, American golfer*

•

More than anything, I must have flowers, always, always.

Claude Monet *1840–1926, French Impressionist artist*

•

He who plants a garden plants happiness.

Anon

Photo: Jonathan Merrell

If you have a garden and a library you have everything you need.

Marcus Tullius Cicero *106 BC–43 BC, Roman statesman and philosopher*

•

A garden is a thing of beauty and a job forever.

Richard Briers *1934–present day, English actor*

•

The true gardener, like an artist, is never satisfied.

H. E. Bates *1905–1974, English writer*

•

God made rainy days so gardeners could get the housework done.

Anon

Tools of the trade

But he said to me, "My grace is sufficient for you..."
2 Corinthians 12:9 (NIV)

Man has always gardened. Initially, he used the most basic of tools. Nowadays though, garden centres and DIY stores try and seduce us with state-of-the-art gadgets we never knew we needed. There are tools for cutting, tools for digging, tools for sowing, all of which our ancestors managed without.

Some people just have to have the latest equipment. Think of *The Good Life's* Margot Ledbetter for instance. Margot, no doubt, would have been incapable of weeding a flower bed without a kneeler, gloves, secateurs, trowels of various sizes, shapes and colours, and a smart gardening hat. The prospect of kneeling on the grass and using her hands would have been unthinkable. (How could anyone possibly weed a garden without all the relevant equipment?)

Often, in our churches, we claim that we haven't the necessary resources to even think about outreach. "We just don't have enough people," we might say. "They're too elderly / too young / too whatever-excuse-we-can-think-of." We might pray fervently for a better-resourced congregation. We may even daydream about what we could do if and when our prayers are answered and we have enough people of 'the right kind'.

But our feeble excuses aren't watertight.

Two thousand years ago, Jesus entrusted seventy-two ordinary individuals to go out and spread the good news of His Father's Kingdom. They travelled in pairs to various places, equipped with nothing more than God's word, the promises of Jesus and the power of the Holy Spirit. That was all they needed to do the job efficiently.

However small or incapacitated our congregation, we can still carry out the tasks God sets us. God never asks us to do something without providing all the resources we need. We will always have his word, Jesus' promise and the power of the Holy Spirit.

There *are* no excuses.

*Sorry Lord, sometimes we forget that your grace is sufficient for us.
Help us to remember that there's nothing more we need, and give us
a gentle prod when we forget. Thank you, Father.*

An established plant becomes an heirloom, for in all likelihood,
it will outlive the gardener who plants it.

Elizabeth Lawrence *1904–1985, American gardening writer*

Sponsors needed

Therefore encourage one another and build each other up, just as in fact you are doing.
1 Thessalonians 5:11 (NIV)

●

Signs are cropping up all over our local roundabouts. *This roundabout has been sponsored by Diddle and Gazump Estate Agents* or *This roundabout has been sponsored by Bob the Building Merchant*. Sponsored to do what, exactly? Swim 100 lengths, cycle 12 miles? I guess it's being sponsored to bloom and grow, and that takes money, green fingers and plenty of encouragement. Our roundabouts are certainly looking lovely, each one looks like a well-tended garden – I feel inspired to ask someone to sponsor my back garden. It needs all the encouragement it can get.

A garden is a friend you can visit anytime. ***Anon***

Of all the leaders in the early church, Barnabas is one I'd love to meet. His real name was Joseph, but the apostles gave him the name "Barnabas" meaning *Son of Encouragement* because he was an encouragement to all who knew him.

First we hear how Barnabas sold a field to help provide food for all those who were converted at Pentecost but who then stayed on in Jerusalem to hear more about Jesus. Later we hear how Barnabas sponsored Paul when he tried to join the believers. Initially Paul was not welcomed into their group since people doubted his conversion and thought his overtures were all part of a cunning plot to arrest the believers. However, once Barnabas spoke up for Paul and introduced him to the group, they were all happy to accept him.

There are times when we all need a sponsor, an encourager who will walk with us, talk with us and point us in the right direction. Godparents, prayer partners and pastors all have sponsorship and encouragement written into their job description, but this is not a task exclusive to a few designated people. We can all encourage others to bloom and grow, whether we give time or money or encouragement. Ask God to point out someone who needs your 'sponsorship' today, it might simply be a question of a timely phone call and a listening ear at the right moment. Ask God to show you what's required.

And remember, plants are a bit like people, you can encourage them with a quick chat too! As Prince Charles once said,

I just come and talk to the plants, really – very important to talk to them, they respond I find. And modern scientific research seems to agree.

Lord, sometimes I'm so wrapped up in my own world that I forget that my friends and family might be in need of support. Open my eyes to someone who needs a little extra encouragement today.

*A perfect summer day is when
the sun is shining,
the breeze is blowing,
the birds are singing,
and the lawn mower is broken.*

James Dent

Gardening TIPS

Drag your finger nails across a bar of soap before you start gardening, then the earth won't go deep down inside and you'll find it easier to clean your hands afterwards.

●

Ants can't climb onto your garden table if you cover the bottom of the legs with Vaseline. Re-apply every couple of weeks or so, depending on rain.

●

Stretch a pair of old tights over the end of the down pipe leading into a water butt to filter out leaves and debris from the incoming water.

●

Put gravel over the top surface of a plant pot to deter slugs and snails and grease the rim with Vaseline.

●

Water late at night and the slugs and snails will come out over night to nibble the damp plant leaves. Water early in the morning to prevent this happening.

●

Add tea bags to the compost heap and pour cold tea on azaleas, rhododendrons and camellias.

Photos: Richard Ward

Compost chaos

The first thing I want you to do is pray.
1 Timothy 2:1 (The Message)

I read a hilarious story in the newspaper recently.

One dark evening, police officers searching for two runaway car thieves broke down a garden gate and smashed their way into a back garden. They charged across the lawn, stumbling over children's toys and the garden trampoline in their haste to arrest two completely unsuspecting *(pause for effect)* compost bins. They were left with egg on their faces… and tea bags, vegetable peelings and rotten fruit too!

Thermal-imaging equipment on board a police helicopter had revealed two glowing images in a south London garden which, in their hurry and misguided enthusiasm, they assumed to be the suspects. It's amazing how much heat can be generated by a compost bin. Fortunately the householders saw the funny side of the incident, as did all the neighbours who were hanging out of their bedroom windows. We all make mistakes every day, tiny mistakes that spoil our day and great big mistakes that spoil our lives and separate us from God. Sometimes we just need to stop and think before we act or speak in order to avoid wrong decisions, hurt feelings and the pointless and often costly mistakes that can mess up lives.

In Sunday School there used to be a picture of a set of traffic lights with the words STOP, PRAY and GO written from top to bottom over the red, amber and green lights. So, if you're the kind of person who jumps in with both wellington boots… remember to stop and pray, however briefly, and then move forward with God.

And if you are too busy to pray, you are TOO busy!

PS: Whatever mistakes you've made in the past, remember that God is in the forgiveness business.

Lord, sometimes life is moving so fast that I don't have time to pray. Help me to organise my days a little better.

This is a replica of a Victorian brick compost bin, created by arranging bricks in gently decreasing circles. Once filled, the compost will be ready in about a year. It looks really attractive, but it can be rather time consuming, since the bricks will have to be dismantled when you want to remove the compost!

Crackpot beauty

Summing it all up, friends, I'd say you'll do best by filling your minds and meditating on things true, noble, reputable, authentic, compelling, gracious – the best, not the worst; the beautiful, not the ugly; things to praise, not things to curse.

Philippians 4:8 (The Message)

●

There is an old Chinese story that never fails to inspire…

There was once an old lady who had to take a long walk every day to fetch water from a nearby stream. She collected the water in two pots that were strung on either end of a long pole that she carried across her shoulders. One of the pots had a small crack in it, but the other was just perfect. At the end of her daily walk she always arrived home with just one and a half pots of water as the cracked pot had slowly dripped out its contents all the way home.

The handsome perfect pot became very big headed about the wonderful job it did, while the cracked pot became more and more miserable.

You'll have to indulge me here – these are pots with thoughts and feelings!

After months and months of failing to return home with a full quota of water the cracked pot finally spoke up,

"I'm so sorry, I don't know why you don't throw me out, I leak so badly that I only ever manage to bring home half the water."

Then the old lady smiled,

"Did you notice that there are flowers on your side of the path, but not on the other pot's side? That's because I have always known about your flaw, so I planted flower seeds on your side of the path, and every day as we return home, you water them. For months I've been picking beautiful fragrant flowers for our kitchen table. Without you being just the way you are, we wouldn't have this beauty to grace our house."

None of us are quite perfect, in fact it's the cracks and flaws we each have that make our lives together so very interesting and rewarding. So look for the best in everyone and everything, and to all the crackpots reading this, have a great day and don't forget to stop and smell the flowers along your path!

Photo: Joseph Proctor

Lord, help us to look for all that's good in every situation and to cheerfully make the best of each new challenge.

Photo: Norma Darey

All things bright and beautiful,
all creatures great and small,
all things wise and wonderful:
the Lord God made them all.

Mrs Cecil Frances Alexander
1818–1895, Irish hymn writer

Every perfect flower, and every stately tree,
Every climbing plant, and every fruitful bush
Sings out, 'Glory to God who made us all.'
A rainbow song of praise to the God of all creation.

Photo: Liz Edwards

How does your garden grow?

All the nations you have made will come and worship before you, Lord; they will bring glory to your name. For you are great and do marvellous deeds; you alone are God.

Psalm 86:9-10 (NIV)

•

Have you noticed that when it comes to borders and flower beds, there are two kinds of gardener? There's the formal gardener who plants selected species and colours in neat regimented rows and symmetrical patterns. Then there's the cottage gardener who goes for the natural look, with a mixture of species and colours growing as and where the seed falls. Both types of flower bed have a beauty all their own.

Have you also noticed that there are two types of worshipper? There are those who prefer a formal service with a high degree of order and discipline. They consider the business of revering God to be a very serious matter. Procedures must be followed carefully and respectfully. And then there are those who prefer a freer, 'go-where-the Spirit-leads-us' type of service, where structure is less important and anyone can share their experience of God's love.

Both kinds of worship are beautiful in different ways. There is no right or wrong. Of course, these are two extremes in patterns of worship, and in reality, most of us would choose somewhere between the two. Sometimes we want – or need – to worship God with solemn reverence. At other times, we feel more spontaneous and enjoy expressing that.

Just as a keen gardener appreciates the various styles of borders and flower beds in every garden he or she visits, God, the Head Gardener, enjoys the variety of colours and tones that we employ to praise him. Our worship is always pleasing in his sight, so let's get on and do it. *AC*

Father, forgive us when we behave as if our style of worship is the only 'proper' way. You love each one of your children and every sincere and heartfelt expression of worship is beautiful to you. Bless you, Father.

Lessons from a tomato plant

When you become fruitful disciples of mine, my Father will be honoured.

John 15:8 (CEV)

●

As a first timer in growing home-grown tomatoes, I was thrilled to see the small pot with green leaves grow to a point where it needed re-potting, and then before too long, re-potting again! I was the expectant parent of scores of tomatoes.

In the process of the excitement, I recognised some very real lessons for life.

This one solitary tomato plant needed regular watering, feeding and gentle pruning to get the best tomatoes. I checked on it daily for weeks on end and developed maternal instincts towards it. Eventually my efforts were rewarded with the tastiest tomatoes I have ever eaten. It was a sad day when I picked the very last one, I felt like a bereft parent!

As Christians, we too need to be watered, pruned and fed, though not with tomato feed but with the word of God, the Bible. And God's concern for us is far greater than mine for the tomato plant.

The tomato plant was reliant upon sunshine, water and food and me checking to make sure it received everything it needed. Christians are reliant upon learning from God's word, fellowship with other believers and prayer. I won't go so far as to say that I talked to my plant, but some say it works. As a Christian, I believe that prayer is the best communication system in the world and it's been around a lot longer than the telephone or internet. The only time it breaks down is when we sever the connection at our end. Unlike my internet connection, which breaks down regularly for no apparent reason.

At the end of the season, I planted out the seeds from my last rosy tomato and now have many seedlings ready for next year.

In life, we are only on this earth for an allotted time, and just as my tomato plant died when it had fulfilled its purpose, so will we. But will we leave behind a legacy?

The Bible says, *"This is to my Father's glory, that you bear much fruit, showing yourselves to be my disciples.'* John 15:8

I hope that others can glimpse my faith by the way I live my life. I want them to know about Jesus and what he has done for us by dying on the cross, defeating death by his resurrection, and offering us a place in heaven with him for eternity. And if my life is fruitful, then perhaps my friends will want to meet The Gardener.

Tomato plants are great teachers!

Lord, it's great to garden with you, to watch things bloom and grow and bear fruit. Please help me to grow closer to you so that those around me can glimpse your love through how I live my life.

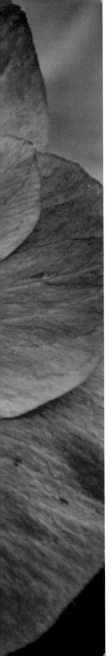

Garden Prayer

Thank you, Lord, that you reveal yourself
in the minute details of creation.
The tiny flower,
the bright ladybird,
the dew drop on a cobweb.
The fragrant scent of a rambling rose,
the rustling leaves of towering trees,
the smooth shine of a new conker.
Lord, I love to spend time gardening with you.
You provide a feast for our senses
and wherever I look,
I see your hand at work.

Photo: Richard Ward

Lifting the burden

Come to me, all you who are weary and burdened, and I will give you rest.

Matthew 11:28 (NIV)

●

It was a lovely sunny Autumn day and I wanted to get outside and enjoy the sunshine. I couldn't think of any other garden job to do, so I spent a happy half hour raking up the leaves on the back lawn. They were cheerful shades of orange and yellow and really looked quite attractive on the ground, but as I raked them up, I realized how much the grass below had been suffering. The lawn visibly stretched as the weight of leaves was lifted and each blade of grass looked up to the sun and breathed a sweet sigh of relief. OK so I'm exaggerating, but the grass does look happier and healthier now that it can enjoy the sunshine!

Sometimes we take on so many jobs in our community, at work or at church that we feel quite burdened and when someone lifts the weight off our shoulders the relief is enormous. At other times, circumstances dictate that we have to carry a huge weight of responsibility on our shoulders. Family illness, needy children, aging relatives, long hours at work or lack of work can all become a burden and even when we carry the load gladly – fatigue soon sets in. If you know someone in those circumstances, reach out a helping hand. Babysit, granny sit, do the shopping, sit with them a while or call them up and offer a listening ear.

And if you are in that situation, be assured that Jesus knows what you are going through and wants to give you rest and fresh strength to cope. Ask him to help you shoulder the burden.

Lord Jesus, thank you that you know every detail of my life and you want to share the burdens. Help me to reach out to others in the same way that you reach out to me.

*Autumn is a season for big
decisions – like whether
or not it's too late to start
spring cleaning.*

Anon

On rocky ground

But Thomas said, "First, I must see the nail scars in his hands and touch
them with my finger. I must put my hand where the spear went into his side.
I won't believe unless I do this!"

John 20:25 (CEV)

Digging a flower bed is hard work. Your
back aches, the sweat runs down your
face and the clay sticks to the spade
or garden fork. And then, to top it all –
clunk! – you strike something hard and
you wonder if it's worth it.

Christianity is not dissimilar to gardening.
We take up Christ's offer and set to work
turning our lives into a garden of faith.
We start out with great enthusiasm, keen
to sow and harvest for God, but before
long we hit a doubt and it's enough to
make us want to pack it all in.

Doubts are like rocks. They come in all
shapes and sizes. Hidden beneath the
surface, a rock may seem as big as a
tractor wheel. But dig down and it may
be just a shallow stone, wafer-thin and
easy to remove. Another time, a stone
may appear as small as a two-pence
piece, but when we start digging it could
be a foot deep and we may need help
to remove it.

Likewise, a niggling doubt could be deep-rooted, whilst a seemingly insurmountable doubt might have a simple explanation.

The thing is, until we investigate, we don't know.

Ignore our doubts, and the sowing and reaping will be hard. But dealing with our doubts, however trivial or deep-rooted, helps us grow as Christians and, once above ground, we can use them, like stones in a rockery, to add a new dimension to our faith. *AC*

Help us, Father, to bring our doubts into the open, and in so doing, to clear the soil of our lives, ready for your love to take root and grow.

Photo: Tim Sandall

The best place to seek God is in a garden. You can dig for him there.
George Bernard Shaw *1856–1950, English playwright*

GARDEN sayings

The best way to garden is to put on a wide-brimmed straw hat and some old clothes. And with a hoe in one hand and a cold drink in the other, tell somebody else where to dig.

Anon

●

Coffee. Garden. Coffee. Does a good morning need anything else?

Betsy Cañas Garmon, American artist and writer

●

What a man needs in gardening is a cast-iron back, with a hinge in it.

Charles Dudley Warner 1829–1900, American novelist

Photo: Tim Fuller

Photo: Joseph Proctor

To dig one's own spade into one's own earth!
Has life anything better to offer than this?

Beverley Nichols 1898–1983, English author and journalist

●

If you want to be happy for a lifetime, plant a garden.

Chinese Proverb

●

You can bury a lot of troubles digging in the dirt.

Anon

TLC transforms

I will bind up the injured and strengthen the weak…

Ezekiel 34:16 (NIV)

●

Whenever I go to a garden centre, I have a tendency to seek out the bargain basement. Here, the weak straggly specimens of the plant world languish unloved and marginalised, with cut-price stickers adorning their pots.

The skinflint in me loves a bargain. I also love the challenge of taking home a poorly plant and nursing it back to health. With a bit of TLC these specimens will flourish. Friends who admire these pampered plants get a potted history (*groan*) of their rags-to-riches transformation.

Some people have a soft spot for wilting weigelas, sickly cyclamen or drooping dahlias. They find fulfilment in tending them and watching them bloom. Other people want only the strongest, hardiest plants, throwing out those that show any sign of weakness. No prizes for guessing the kind of gardener God is!

God loves to rescue the weaker human specimens. He cares deeply about the strong too, but he seeks out the marginalised of society in keeping with his promise made in Ezekiel. *I will search for the lost and bring back the strays. I will bind up the injured and strengthen the weak...* Ezekiel 34:16 (NIV)

Perhaps you remember picking teams at school. The captains would choose the best players first; keen to field the strongest team. Those who weren't athletic would droop awkwardly, hoping that this time they wouldn't be last.

In God's kingdom, all that is turned on its head. Jesus came to seek the weak, the lost and the unloved people of his day. As his followers, we are called to do the same; to speak out for the oppressed, stand up for the weak and fight for the basic human rights of all people. God never gives up on a 'lost cause'. He rescues the weak, and with his tender loving care, they flourish and bloom in his kingdom. *AC*

Lord, thank you for your tender loving care for all people, strong and weak. Help us to look out for the lost and lonely and to bring them to you to be restored.

I will restore your soul

You let me rest in fields of green grass. You lead me to streams of
peaceful water, and you refresh my life.

Psalm 23:2-3 (CEV)

Photo: Ian Strachan – Monet's garden at Giverny, France

Some while ago, I spent a few days in hospital, although it wasn't me that was unwell. My daughter was put on the children's ward and I stayed in with her. She was placed in solitary confinement in an isolation ward. There was a chance of something contagious and you can't be too careful. The room itself was really rather dull. Not quite a cell, but you get the picture. However, just beyond the window was the most delightful garden.

There were multi-coloured fence posts and seats in fun shapes, a tall curvy mirror hidden in the flower bed, evergreen shrubs and interesting paths, two or three shady trees, ride-ons for the little ones and a special chat-corner just for teenagers.

The garden designer had been really creative; thought about the garden from every angle and considered patients, visitors and children of all ages. It was an imaginative, colourful garden. It was a place to escape to when the four walls of the hospital closed in. A place to breathe fresh air, far away from the antiseptic smell of the ward. A place to restore your soul and revive your spirit. A place that would grow, change and blossom. A place where you could talk to and listen to God.

When God created his first garden in Eden and filled it with good, green, growing things, he knew that this garden would be the first of many. Gardens can be places of tranquillity, new life, rest, relaxation and restoration. When God created people he made them to be creative in his image and he knew that many of them would just love gardening. Gardens and gardening can be a wonderful antidote to stress, fatigue and even illness – everyone should have the opportunity to escape to somewhere green when the need arises.

God created the green spaces to give us a place where we could feel that much closer to him. Genesis reveals that God walked in the Garden of Eden in the cool of the evening, so why not take a stroll around a garden near you and perhaps you could ask God to walk with you.

Lord, when the walls close in help me to find a special place where I can breathe fresh air and meet with you.

Gardening TIPS

Pot marigolds include a natural insect repellent, which protects the plants close by.

Put a layer of newspaper strips in the bottom of a trench and under the compost where you want to plant beans. This will help the soil to retain its moisture by stopping the water draining away too fast.

Plant your seedlings in the late afternoon as the day is cooling down. The young roots will enjoy the warm soil without the full sun scorching their leaves as they get used to their new surroundings.

Use chopped up banana skins as compost under roses. The plant skins include phospates, calcium, sulphur, silica, sodium and magnesium, which will help your roses grow.

Keep birds away from fruit trees by placing tinsel on the branches, or hang old CDs on lengths of cotton. The free CDs that come in the weekend newspapers are ideal!

Pretend snakes can deter birds from eating your fruit – use a child's plastic snake or a coiled length of hose.

Keep birds away from eating your new seeds by placing toy windmills in the flower beds.

Weed-obsessed

When the wheat sprouted and formed ears, then the weeds also appeared.
Matthew 13:26 (NIV)

A few years ago we had a problem with bindweed. It took root the other side of our boundary and made midnight raids under the fence to claim more territory. At least it seemed that way. I'd spend ages pulling up the pesky plant, only for it to reappear stronger and healthier days later.

My fight with this creeping menace became an obsession. I'd go into the garden to see how the bindweed was doing and barely notice the flowers and shrubs I'd lovingly planted just months before. I neglected to deadhead the roses and feed the patio plants. I ignored the birdsong and butterflies as I concentrated on my quest to eradicate the enemy.

Weeds flourish in most gardens. And evil flourishes in our fallen world. It seems that however hard we try to keep it at bay, it's always one step ahead. It's all too easy to overlook the good things in life as we get sidetracked by negative news in our papers and on TV.

Photo: Tony Bagwell

What is a weed? A plant whose virtues have not yet been discovered.
Ralph Waldo Emerson 1803–1882, American lecturer and writer

Photo: Tim Fuller

Some folk are always ready to discuss bad news! They even search it out and fuel the widespread view that today's world is a terrible place in which to live. That's a shame – they are missing so much.

God created a beautiful world. He adorned it with a vast array of amazing animals and plant life, incredible sights, sounds, textures and aromas. There is so much that's awe-inspiring all around us, so let's focus on the positive rather than dwell on the negative.

We must stand up against evil, certainly, but we must also seek out and promote the good things in life and give thanks to God for his glorious, joyous Creation and for one another.

Forgive us, Father, for our tendency to dwell on the negative.
Open our hearts and senses to the beauty of your creation,
that we may share our delight with all we meet.

My neighbour asked if he could use my lawnmower and I told him of course he could, so long as he didn't take it out of my garden. *Anon*

Good old grass

Love is patient, love is kind. It does not envy, it does not boast, it is not proud. It is not rude, it is not self-seeking, it is not easily angered, it keeps no record of wrongs.

1 Corinthians 13:4-5 (NIV))

●

Somebody once said, 'The greatest thing about a fall of snow is that it makes my lawn look just as nice as the one next door!' And that's certainly true for my back garden, the grass generally does look greener on the other side of the fence, but that's because our neighbours are a highly mow-tivated couple and they take far more time and trouble over their lush green carpet.

Some good friends were so amused by their own neighbours' efforts to create the perfect lawn that they crept round under cover of darkness and left three small mounds of fresh earth across the middle of the grass – the exact replica of a mole trail! Fortunately, the green-fingered neighbour wasn't too for-lawn, he saw the funny side of the joke and told the tale against himself at many a dinner party.

English lawns are very long-suffering. We water them so they grow and then as soon as they do, we give them a short back and sides, crazy really. We walk all over our grass and even lie on top of it, but it always springs back into shape without bearing a grudge. Good old reliable grass. It's very forgiving and makes very little fuss.

We humans could learn a lot from grass! How much time do we waste nursing hurt feelings, or chewing over a supposed wrong when it would be a happier, healthier option to pick ourselves up, dust ourselves down and get on with living life to the full? Life's too short to keep a list of wrongs. And I'm very glad that when we ask God to forgive our wrongdoing, he not only forgives, but forgets and moves on.

Lord, help us to forget the times when people have hurt our feelings or injured our pride. Show us again how to forgive, forget and move on. We keep forgetting how to do it.

If created things are so utterly lovely,
how gloriously beautiful must he be who made them!
The wisdom of the worker is revealed in his handiwork.

Anthony of Padua
1195–1231, Franciscan Friar

For all things were created by him,
and all things exist through him and for him.
To God be the glory for ever! Amen

Romans 11:36 (GNB)

Photo: Ian Strachan

A fresh perspective

...my power is made perfect in weakness.
2 Corinthians 12:9 (NIV)

●

It had rained overnight and the dew lay heavy on the ground. The garden looked especially vibrant. Yellow, pink and white flowers were displayed to perfection against varying shades of green.

If I hadn't been aware of the smudge on the lens of my glasses I wouldn't have removed them to clean, and I'd have missed the glittering exhibition in the long grass. As it was, I noticed a tiny flickering orange light. With my far-from-perfect eyesight it looked like a tiny dandelion clock and, as I moved my head slightly, it changed colour –

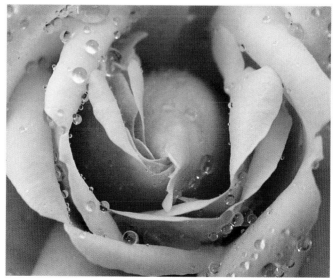

Photo: Richard Ward

God saw all that he had made, and it was very good.
Psalm 1:31 (NIV)

Photo: Richard Ward

yellow…green…blue... Glancing round I saw several lights, all changing colour before my eyes. Fascinated, I put my glasses back on and the lights disappeared, leaving only the dew sparkling white upon the grass.

It was only when I removed my specs again that I could see the colours refracted in each tiny drop of moisture. Who'd have thought that it had taken me a lifetime to notice this glorious display? The conditions had to be right of course – light coming from a certain angle for a start – but it was a joy to discover something new, something that had occurred before but which, with my corrected vision, I had been oblivious to.

We are so used to seeing what we expect to see, and to see it in our own strength. Sometimes we need to 'become weak' in order to be able to see things anew. There is, as I discovered, beauty in weakness.

God has much to show us in the natural world and in life in general. Often that means viewing the world differently, through the eyes of the Creator. Sometimes that means becoming weak – letting go of our egos and our positions of strength in order to view things from an angle of God's choosing.

It takes courage but it's more than worth the risk.

Lord God, give us courage to lay aside our egos and desire for worldly perfection in order that we may see the world afresh, through your eyes.

Basking in the son-light

We must keep our eyes on Jesus, who leads us and makes our faith complete.

Hebrews 12:2 (CEV)

Did you know that plants move? OK they don't exactly get up and walk out of the flower bed when no one's looking, but they do move.

We've had a pot of miniature daffodils on our kitchen windowsill for some weeks now. Every morning I turn the pot so that the flowers face into the room. How is it that a couple of days later they seem to be looking out of the window again? Is someone moving the pot when I'm not looking? No, the daffodil heads are slowly moving round to face the sun. Granted they're not moving fast, but they are definitely moving.

Just as flowers turn to face the sun, so Christians can choose to face the Son. If we want to reflect Jesus' love in our lives, we need to keep our eyes on him and focus on his teaching, then our lives will bloom and grow.

And do you have those nifty, solar-powered lights in your garden? Aren't they clever? We bought a set last year. All day long they are charged up by the power of the sun so that all night long they can shine in the darkness. Think how much power we could absorb from the Son and for how long we might shine his light in the darkness, if we simply turn towards God and focus on his Son, Jesus. *JM*

Lord Jesus, help us to focus on you and then to share the light of your love with those we know.

The LORD bless you and keep you; the LORD make his face shine upon you and be gracious to you; the LORD turn his face towards you and give you peace.

Numbers 6:24-26 (NIV)

There is a garden in every childhood, an enchanted place where colours are brighter, the air softer, and the morning more fragrant than ever again.

Elizabeth Lawrence, 1904–1985, American gardening writer

Variety is the spice of life

Take care of God's needy people and welcome strangers into your home.

Romans 12:13 (CEV)

•

Up until a few years ago, it was frowned upon to have weeds trespassing amongst cultivated plants. It was a sign of a lazy or negligent gardener. You certainly weren't 'keeping up with the Joneses' if you had a stinging nettle in your border! Nowadays, of course, we've seen the light and it's all the rage to have a designated nettle patch. We're eco-friendly and conservation-minded.

We've learnt the hard way. Only through the absence of butterflies and bees and other small creatures have we learned to give time and space to this prolific 'weed'. We all love to see butterflies flitting from flower to flower. There's something other-worldly about these delicate insects with their silent colourful wings and I feel privileged when butterflies visit my garden.

Most people would rather have nettles and butterflies than no nettles and no butterflies. Yes, stinging nettles do sting (it says so on the tin) but handled with care, the pros outnumber the cons.

What can we learn about our church life from this? Well, in theory, of course we want to see everyone coming to church. We want all people to know the saving love of Christ and to experience the joy of being reconciled to God. But in practise, we often prefer to be surrounded by folk with whom we have plenty in common. We want people of a similar background, class and education to our existing friends. An 'arm's length' welcome is often all we offer to those who don't match the type. Shocking isn't it?

And then we wonder why we don't grow! We wonder why we don't enjoy God's rich blessings in all their fullness.

It's when we truly welcome the marginalised, the unpopular and the unloved into our fellowships that we see God's transforming love in action. God's grace, like a butterfly, alights upon those we find hard to love and everyone enjoys the benefits.

AC

Lord, we are a fickle bunch. But we have no right to choose where and whom we're planted with. Each plant, each person is created by you and loved by you. Help us to love as you love; equally, unconditionally.

*A garden is an awful
responsibility. You never
know what you may be aiding
to grow in it.*

Charles Dudley Warner

GARDEN sayings

When weeding, the best way to make sure you are removing a weed and not a valuable plant is to pull on it. If it comes out of the ground easily, it is a valuable plant.

Anon

●

But a weed is simply a plant that wants to grow where people want something else. In blaming nature, people mistake the culprit. Weeds are people's idea, not nature's.

Anon

●

They know, they just know where to grow, how to dupe you, and how to camouflage themselves among the perfectly respectable plants; they just know, and therefore, I've concluded weeds must have brains."

Dianne Benson, *Dirt: The Lowdown on Growing a Garden with Style, 1994*

●

A modest garden contains, for those who know how to look and wait, more instruction than a library.

Anon

●

A garden is the best alternative therapy.

Germaine Greer *1939–present day, Australian-born writer*

●

A weed is a plant that has mastered every survival skill except for learning how to grow in rows. A flower is an educated weed.

Luther Burbank *1849–1926, botanist*

Waiting patiently

For the revelation awaits an appointed time… Though it linger wait for it;
it will certainly come and will not delay.
Habakkuk 2:3 (NIV)

●

It was early spring. I was working in the garden, moving a pile of old bricks rescued from when we repaved the driveway. Hidden in a space between two of the bricks I found a dusty, grey cocoon. Last autumn a caterpillar had fattened itself up by eating into my shrubbery. It had found somewhere to hide, spun its protection against the winter – and hibernated.

As I looked at it, it seemed dead, totally inert with nothing happening. But in the secrecy of the cocoon, changes were taking place. Gradually, quietly, mysteriously, the caterpillar inside was being transformed. In a few days, the restrictive cocoon would split and a new creature would emerge. A butterfly or moth – I can't identify cocoons – would unfold its wings and fly into a freedom it had never known, its waiting time over.

I wonder sometimes about what really happened on the first Easter Saturday. I know about the drama of Good Friday and the joy of Easter Sunday, but what about the day in between? The day when nothing seemed to be happening. The day the disciples were mourning for what had been and didn't yet know what would be.

Photo: Liz Edwards

Even then, things were happening unseen and unknown in the cocoon of God's purposes. Events that would shake the world and change it more powerfully than anything else, events that would give us the freedom to live as nothing else could. All that was needed was time.

Waiting can be hard, but little happens without it.

By Eddie Askew, taken from *Talking with Hedgehogs*

Lord, let me glimpse your purpose in the mystery of life.
And when the mist descends, help me to wait in patience.

Photo: Richard Ward

Growth takes time. Be patient. And while you're waiting, pull a weed.
Emilie Barnes, *American writer and speaker*

One is nearer God's heart in a garden than anywhere else on earth.

Dorothy Frances Gurney
1858–1932, English poet and hymn writer